HORSING
AROUND

# Steeplechase

## Martha Martin

## Crabtree Publishing Company

www.crabtreebooks.com

# Crabtree Publishing Company
www.crabtreebooks.com

**Author:** Martha Martin
**Editor:** Lynn Peppas
**Proofreader:** Crystal Sikkens
**Editorial director:** Kathy Middleton
**Production coordinator:** Katherine Berti
**Prepress technician:** Katherine Berti
**Coordinating editor:** Chester Fisher
**Series editor:** Sue Labella
**Project manager:** Kumar Kunal (Q2AMEDIA)
**Art direction:** Dibakar Acharjee (Q2AMEDIA)
**Cover design:** Shruti Aggarwal (Q2AMEDIA)
**Design:** Ritu Chopra (Q2AMEDIA)
**Photo research:** Ekta Sharma (Q2AMEDIA)
**Reading consultant:** Cecilia Minden, Ph.D.

**Cover:** Adam Trinder riding Swift Rule jumps a hurdle during the Cleanevent Grand National Steeplechase in Melbourne, Australia.

**Title page:** Riders exercise steeplechase horses.

**Photographs:**
Cover: Quinn Rooney/Getty Images (main image), Emberiza/Shutterstock, Tischenko Irina/Shutterstock, P1: Robert Hallam/Rex Features, P4: Paul A. Souders/Corbis, P5: Allan Kilgour/Shutterstock, P6: Christie's Images/Corbis, P7: Bob Langrish, P8: Nigel Roddis/Reuters, P9: Mike Hewitt/Getty Images, P10: Paul Thompson Images/Alamy, P11: Mikhail Kondrashov/Fotolia, P12: Bob Langrish, P13: Bob Langrish, P14: Robert Hallam/Rex Features, P15: Lesley Rigg/Bigstockphoto, P16: Jon Super/Associated Press, P17: Brett Charlton/Istockphoto, P18: Rex Features, P19: Julian Finney/Getty Images, P20: Petr Josek Snr/Reuters, P21: Bob Langrish, P22: Snap/Rex Features, P23: Kit Houghton/Corbis, P24: Peter Price/Rex Features, P25: John Morris/Alamy, P26: Trinity Mirror/Mirrorpix/Alamy, P27: Popperfoto/Getty Images, P28: David Crump/Rex Features, P29: Rex Features, P30: Rui Vieira/Associated Press, P31: Warren Little/Getty Images, Folio Image: Wendy Kaveney Photography/Shutterstock

**Library and Archives Canada Cataloguing in Publication**

Martin, Martha, 1967-
   Steeplechase / Martha Martin.

(Horsing around)
Includes index.
ISBN 978-0-7787-4981-3 (bound).--ISBN 978-0-7787-4997-4 (pbk.)

   1. Steeplechasing--Juvenile literature. I. Title. II. Series: Horsing around (St. Catharines, Ont.)

SF359.M37 2009      j798.4'5      C2009-904186-3

**Library of Congress Cataloging-in-Publication Data**

Martin, Martha, 1967-
  Steeplechase / Martha Martin.
    p. cm. -- (Horsing around)
  Includes index.
  ISBN 978-0-7787-4997-4 (pbk. : alk. paper) -- ISBN 978-0-7787-4981-3
(reinforced library binding : alk. paper)
  1. Steeplechasing--Juvenile literature. I. Title. II. Series.

SF359.M37 2010
798.4'5--dc22

2009027265

**Crabtree Publishing Company**
www.crabtreebooks.com    1-800-387-7650
Copyright © **2010 CRABTREE PUBLISHING COMPANY**. All rights reserved. No part of this publication may be reproduced, stored in a retrieval system or be transmitted in any form or by any means, electronic, mechanical, photocopying, recording, or otherwise, without the prior written permission of Crabtree Publishing Company. In Canada: We acknowledge the financial support of the Government of Canada through the Book Publishing Industry Development Program (BPIDP) for our publishing activities.

**Published in Canada**
**Crabtree Publishing**
616 Welland Ave.
St. Catharines, ON
L2M 5V6

**Published in the United States**
**Crabtree Publishing**
PMB16A
350 Fifth Ave., Suite 3308
New York, NY 10118

**Published in the United Kingdom**
**Crabtree Publishing**
Maritime House
Basin Road North, Hove
BN41 1WR

**Published in Australia**
**Crabtree Publishing**
386 Mt. Alexander Rd.
Ascot Vale (Melbourne)
VIC 3032

# Contents

# Steeplechase 101

In some parts of Europe, Steeplechase is also called National Hunt racing. In this race, steeplechase winners need speed, strength, and courage to get to the finish line. They also have to be great jumpers!

A timber racer needs the same jumping skills as a steeplechaser, even though the fences aren't as high.

Steeplechase jumps are called fences. These fences are at least 4.5 feet (1.35 m) tall. They are solid jumps. Solid jumps do not move when a horse hits them, causing the horse to fall as a result. Streams and ditches are also part of some races. Hurdle racing is a type of steeplechase. In hurdle racing, the race is shorter. The distance is between 1 and 2 miles long (1.6–3.3 km). Hurdles are not as high as fences. They are not solid. Jumps that are not solid move easily when a horse hits them, and the horse will most likely not fall. The Cheltenham Gold Cup is the most famous hurdle race in England.

Jumping over shorter fences and hedges is good training for the real thing.

Timber racing is another kind of steeplechase. It began in the United States. In timber races, horses jump wooden fences made of crossed poles. The track is between 3 to 4 miles long (about 5 to 6 km). One of the most famous timber races is the Maryland Hunt Cup. It started in 1894.

The racers' real skills come through when taking a jump. One wrong move or bad timing means trouble. The horse and rider can crash into the fence. They could even crash into another horse! Many **jockeys** fall or are knocked off. Both the horse and jockey can be harmed in steeplechase.

## FACT BOX

Did you know steeplechase racers can have two legs as well as four? The name "steeplechase" is also used to describe human racers who leap over hurdles around a special track.

# Steeplechase History

Many people think steeplechase started in Ireland in the 1700s. According to one legend, two Irish riders raced four miles (6 km) across the countryside. They wanted to see who had the fastest horse. They used church steeples as markers because riders could see them from far away. Steeples are tall, pointed structures that were often on churches.

No one knows for sure how steeplechase really began. By the 1800s, it was very popular. Foxhunters used it to keep their horses in shape when they were not hunting. Steeplechase races were often part of hunting events. Horses leaped over whatever was in their path. It could be hedges, fences, or creeks.

The artist John Sanderson-Wells captured this moment of steeplechase history at Becher's Brook back in the 1800's.

Foxhunting still goes on in many countries today—but you won't find steeplechasers on the hunting fields.

Each rider took his own path. Sometimes racers made holes in the hedges ahead of time. Then they didn't have to jump! Today steeplechase is one of the fastest growing sports in the world.

It is enjoyed by everyone from children to royalty. Steeplechase has become big business. Many people gamble on the races. They bet on the horse and rider they believe will come in first. This betting has been around since steeplechase started.

7

# The Grand National

The Steeplechase Grand National was first held in 1839. Its barriers included two hurdles and a stone wall. Today, the most famous steeplechase race in the world is the John Smith's Grand National. It takes place in Aintree, England.

In 1843, the Grand National became a **handicap** race. The best horses were "handicapped." This means they had to carry more weight. That made the race more evenly matched. Today, the Grand National is held every year in April. The soft and springy ground is perfect for jumping. A large group of horses race twice around a turf track. The total distance is four miles and four **furlongs** (over 7 km).

Horses and riders race around the Aintree track, competing for the best position.

There are 16 fences on the track at Aintree. The horses go around the track once, jumping all 16. Then they repeat the first 14 fences, and end on a long flat run. Sometimes the fences have ditches before or after them. This adds to the challenge. The Grand National is one of the most-watched sporting events in the world. In 2009, the purse was worth £ 900,000 or over one million U.S. dollars. The total prize money from the entire three-day meeting at Aintree totaled more than four million U.S. dollars!

### FACT BOX
Did you know many horses continue to run during a steeplechase, even if their jockeys fall, or are knocked off? A number of them also leap over the jumps!

Riderless horses continue to compete at Aintree's Grand National.

# The Thoroughbreds

The thoroughbred is the only breed allowed to race in England's famous Grand National Steeplechase. Thoroughbred horses are often called Hotbloods. This name is also used by their cousin, the Arabian horse. This is because their ancestors came from the hot climate countries of the East.

The ancestors of a thoroughbred horse must include one of three famous Arabian **stallions**. These are known as The Foundation **Sires**. These three stallions were brought to England between 1680 and 1729. They were matched with the strongest, fastest English **mares**. The breeders hoped to create the perfect horse by mixing the breeds.

James Weatherby was one of the early members of the English Jockey Club. He recorded the ancestors of all the race horses in England in the 1700's. The Jockey Club then published his results in the "General Stud Book" (or "GSB") in 1791. The book has been kept up to date ever since.

HYPERION
1930 - 1960

The Jockey Club in Newmarket, England is a great stop for horse-loving tourists today.

This British thoroughbred loves to play and prance on his days off.

A horse cannot race in a professional steeplechase if it is not listed in the "GSB." Thoroughbreds are known for their long, sloping shoulders. They have graceful, arched necks. These horses also have muscular hindquarters. They have strong legs and athletic ability. They can be any solid color. Thoroughbreds are between 15 and 17 **hands** tall (about 1.5 to 1.7 m). A horse's height is measured from the ground to the horse's **withers**. Thoroughbreds take part in sports such as polo, dressage, and all kinds of horse races.

### FACT BOX

"Thoroughbreds" are also popular in stories! The book series, *Thoroughbred*, began in 1991. The original author, Joanna Campbell, had over 72 titles in print before the series ended in 2005. You can still find them in some book stores and libraries today!

11

# Making a Winner

Steeplechase horses are not just born winners. They come from a long line of carefully selected parents. They then go through years of training and proper care. This helps them end up in the winner's circle.

Some horses are worth a lot of money before they're even born. Breeders can spend a fortune making sure their new foals have the best **bloodlines**. Still, good bloodlines don't always mean a winner. It takes time to see if a young thoroughbred has what it takes to be a steeplechase racehorse.

Thoroughbreds usually begin training when they are yearlings, or a year old. Often owners pay to have someone else train their horses. They may even send the horse away to be trained.

Young foals are worth a great deal of money if their bloodlines are good.

First, horses learn to work with each piece of equipment. This might be the saddle and bridle. Then the young horse has to get used to having a rider on its back. Once the horse has learned the basics, the trainer can work on flat-racing skills. Trainers work on different **gaits** such as trotting, cantering, and galloping. Finally, trainers work on jumping skills. Horses must be at least three years old to race in steeplechase. This gives the horse years to practice. Trainers work with horses to keep them in perfect health. Horses are given many vitamins and minerals. This keeps them strong and fit.

### FACT BOX

It is easy to keep track of a thoroughbred's age. In North America or Great Britain, it does not matter what day a foal is born. Its birthday is always recorded as January 1 of that year.

*A young steeplechaser has to start out small when she's learning to jump.*

13

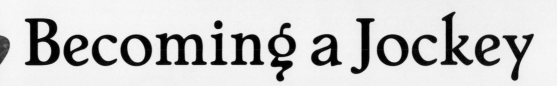

# Becoming a Jockey

A good jockey is a big part of a steeplechase winner's success. A person doesn't become a jockey overnight, though. Training and experience are needed.

A jockey needs to know horses. A person might start as a volunteer at a well-run stable or training center. Experienced trainers or jockeys may act as **mentors** and give helpful suggestions. Many jockeys begin by working as stable hands. In time, they may become grooms. With experience, they move on to become exercise riders. If they are any good, they enroll in schooling races. These races are used to teach both the horse and jockey the skills they'll need in an official race.

Exercise riders have the important job of keeping the horses in good shape by walking them every day.

In order to race professionally, a jockey must have a license. In most countries, jockeys need to be 18 years old before they can qualify for their license. Jockey schools and training programs are around the world. They help jockeys earn their licenses.

Jockeys can also apply for a license without the official training. A jockey needs to have an apprentice jockey license for a year. An apprentice is one who is learning. Then he or she can apply for a journeyman jockey's license.

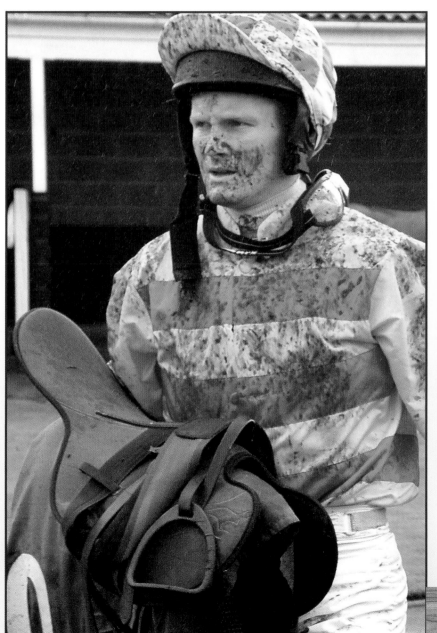

### FACT BOX

The youngest jockey ever to win the Grand National was Bruce Hobbs in 1938. He was 17 years old. The oldest jockey ever to win the Grand National was Dick Saunders in 1982. He was 48 years old. It was the only time he competed in a Grand National.

*Being a steeplechase jockey is a very messy job.*

# Tools of the Trade

Both thoroughbreds and their jockeys wear special equipment in steeplechase. The equipment keeps the horse and rider safe and comfortable. This is important in the exciting and dangerous world of racing.

*Good protective clothing on a jockey can mean the difference between a safe ride, and a serious injury.*

A jockey is known by his "silks." This is the name given to the brightly-colored uniform each jockey wears on race day. Each jockey wears different color combinations. The colors are chosen by the horse's owner and trainer. Some people believe this tradition goes back to medieval times, when knights wore the colors of their lords in tournaments.

Everyone can tell who is in the lead based on their colored silks. A jockey also needs a hard hat, goggles, and high boots. Jockeys today must wear a special padding under their silks. This helps the jockey stay as safe from injury as possible.

shadow roll

A shadow roll helps a horse by limiting its view of shadows that might spook it.

Thoroughbreds must wear certain **tack** to keep them safe. Special racing saddles are small and light. Some horses wear protective boots called splint boots. They protect the lower part of the horse's leg. A bridle, halter, reins, and stirrups are still used but are specially made for steeplechase. For example, rubber reins are recommended. Some trainers also use double bridles, **shadow rolls**, and **martingales**. These all help keep horses safe and race their best.

### FACT BOX

Long ago jockeys and horses did not have any special equipment for steeplechase racing. They just wore their regular foxhunting or riding clothes. There were many injuries!

# Risks of Steeplechase

Steeplechase isn't all fun and games. It's one of the most dangerous horse sports around. Injuries happen to both horses and riders. That is nothing to "horse around" about!

Many horses died because of steeplechase races. Horses don't always die at the actual races. Sometimes they have to be euthanized because of injuries they got while racing. The jumps are usually the cause of the most serious accidents. Thirty horses died at Aintree between 1998 and 2008 alone. A number of jockeys have also been injured in steeplechase.

*Sometimes the safest way to avoid injury is to jump free of your horse.*

According to a study done on steeplechase at the University of Liverpool, certain things increase the chances of serious injuries. Sunlight on race day seems to have a bad effect on some horses. Scientists are not sure exactly why. Some horses have to make long trips to get to the races. Risks are higher if they don't get an overnight rest. Young horses have more injuries than older horses. Easily excited animals get hurt more often.

A track that is too-firm will add to injuries. Because of the dangers, people continue to protest steeplechase around the world. Officials have made a number of safety changes. A jump at Becher's Brook at Aintree no longer has a ditch. This makes the jump safer. Officials have added new safety rules. These include making jockeys wear protective body gear. Still, steeplechase injuries continue.

### FACT BOX

In 2001, the largest British animal rights organization, Animal Aid, declared that the Grand National at Aintree was illegal. The organization used the 1911 Protection of Animal Act to support this. So far, the legal system hasn't said if they're right or wrong.

Falling off your horse can cause injuries, but so can other horses landing on top of you. Rolling clear is the best option for safety if you fall.

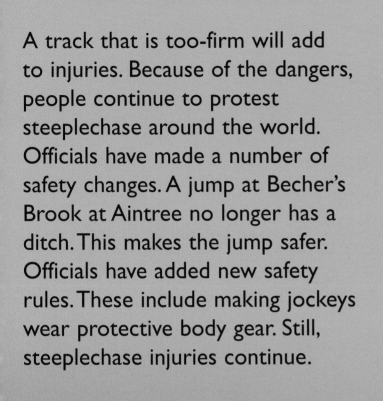

# Steeplechase Language

The world of horse racing has its own language. You may hear some phrases in everyday speech. Some words people hear only at the track. In order to appreciate steeplechase, you need to speak the language!

There are certain words used in steeplechase all the time. A "chaser" is the name given to any steeplechase racehorse. A "punter" is someone who bets on a race. This is similar to a gambler in horse racing. A "hunter" was traditionally the name given to a horse that was used in a hunt.

Sometimes a steeplechase is won, quite literally, "by a nose!"

Now, a "hunter" means any horse that is strong, fast, and a great jumper. A "stayer" has what it takes to finish the race! Someone who is training horses might say they need to "pony the racehorse." This means a horse with a rider would use a lead so the racehorse follows them. The term comes from flat racing, where a rider on a pony often led the racehorse to the starting gate. Sometimes a horse needs "hot walking." This means the horse is hot and needs to be cooled down after a race by walking. Sometimes people say horses need to be "walked hot" before the race. This really means "to warm them up."

### FACT BOX

Some horse expressions have become everyday language. Take the expression "long in the teeth." As a horse gets older, his teeth keep growing. Human teeth don't. An old horse has long teeth—so an older person is "long in the tooth!"

Horse's teeth need proper care. Often it's necessary to file the teeth to make them shorter and even. This is known as "floating."

# 10 National Velvet

There are many movies with horses in them. You know you will see many horses in Westerns. When Hollywood decided to focus on steeplechase, one movie made history.

The movie, *National Velvet*, is based on the 1935 book by Enid Baghold. It was filmed in 1944 and won two Academy Awards. It starred Elizabeth Taylor, a famous actress. Taylor was only 12 years old when she was cast as the main character, Velvet Brown. In the movie, Velvet convinces her father to keep the badly behaved horse, Pirate. Velvet is sure "The Pie" can win the Grand National at Aintree if she trains him right.

Terry Kilburn, Elizabeth Taylor, Mickey Rooney, and "King Charles" are still famous today for the movie, *National Velvet*.

At the last minute, Velvet decides to dress up as a boy. Then she quickly takes the place of Pie's regular jockey in the big race.

In 1960, Hollywood created a T.V. show based on the movie. It lasted for two years. The young girl who played Velvet dyed her hair black. She needed to make herself look more like Elizabeth Taylor. It helped her get the job. In 1978, Hollywood made a sequel to *National Velvet*. It was called *International Velvet*. Velvet's niece, Sarah, comes from Arizona to live with her aunt and uncle in England. Sarah ends up with one of "The Pie's" foals.

**FACT BOX**

In the movie, *National Velvet*, the horse's background and origins are never given. Since his bloodlines aren't known, he couldn't be in the General Stud Book. That means "The Pie" wouldn't be permitted to race in the Grand National in real life!

She names it Arizona Pie. She and her horse compete for England in the Olympic Three Day Event and win gold.

*Jockeys clear a jump at The Grand National at Aintree in England.*

# Red Rum: Superstar

One of the most famous chasers was an Irish-born thoroughbred named Red Rum. His first race was in Liverpool in 1966. A bone disease almost finished his career in 1972. He still went on to make steeplechase history.

*Red Rum loved being the center of attention. He enjoyed his frequent public appearances.*

24

In 1972, Red Rum got a new owner. Donald "Ginger" McCain wanted to see what his new racehorse could do. He took Rummy out on the beach near his stable. Ginger was shocked to see Rummy move like he was lame. It turned out Red Rum had a bone disease in his hooves! Over the next few months, Rummy's trainer raced him on the firm sandy beach. Then he soaked the horse's feet in the cool saltwater. By April 1973, Red Rum was in great shape for the Grand National.

Rummy began the race in 12th place, but he finished in first in 9 minutes and 1.9 seconds. Red Rum went on to win the Grand National the next year, too.

This bronze statue of Red Rum stands at Aintree as a memorial to the greatest Grand National champion.

In 1977, he won a third time. He was the only horse to do so. Rummy was twelve years old. In 1979, Red Rum retired. In 1988, he was invited to Aintree where he was honored with a statue.

When he died at the age of 30, he was buried beside the finish line at Aintree. Here fans still visit and honor him. Red Rum was a special horse. He overcame illness to bring steeplechase its greatest glory.

**FACT BOX**

The bone disease that affected Red Rum's hooves is called Pedalostitis. It means "inflammation of the pedal," which is a small bone in the horse's foot. It is very painful, and can make a horse lame if it is not treated.

# More Great Horse Tales

The sport of steeplechase is full of fabulous horse tales. Red Rum is perhaps the best known steeplechase superstar. There are some other fine thoroughbreds who have also made history.

The winner of the Grand National in 1967 was named Foinavon. Foinavon was a well-known horse in the history of racing because nobody thought he could ever win. He gave everyone a big surprise!

Foinavon and the other horses were on their second loop at Aintree. Some of the horses were without their riders. When they got to a smaller fence, they didn't jump. The horses that followed them were spooked by this.

*Foinavon and his jockey are the perfect example of teamwork. They worked together to win the race!*

The next group of horses had to slow down because of the confusion. Some of them lost their jockeys. Foinavon was coming up from the rear. His rider saw what was happening. He led Foinavon around the mob. They made it over that fence on the first try. This lead was just what they needed to win the race!

Esha Ness is known as the horse who won the "National That Wasn't." In 1993, the Grand National had a number of false starts. Some of the jockeys didn't know the last start was false. They kept racing. Esha Ness and his jockey crossed the finish line first. That is when they learned the race didn't count!

**FACT BOX**

The Wild Man of Borneo won the Grand National in 1895. When he died, his owner had the stallion's head stuffed! It hung for years on the wall at Aintree.

The Wild Man of Borneo ran the Grand National a total of four times. He won it in 1895, on his second attempt.

# 13 Riding Superstars

Steeplechase superstars need talented trainers and jockeys. A number of human heroes have become world famous in steeplechase history.

In the early days of the sport, there were great characters such as Captain Becher. In 1839, he fell off his horse at a fence. The story says that he ducked under the water while the other horses leaped over him! Today, that fence is called Becher's Brook.

Jenny Pitman is a training hero. She was the first female trainer to have a Grand National winner in 1983. Her horse was named Corbiere. She made history again when she repeated her success in 1995.

Bob Champion is one of the most famous human heroes of steeplechase. In 1979, he learned he had cancer.

*Bob Champion and his horse, Aldaniti, were both underdogs. Their win brought the crowds to their feet.*

Doctors gave him only eight months to live. Champion fought back with the doctors' help. In 1981, he entered the Grand National again. This time he rode a horse named Aldaniti. The horse was also a survivor. He had battled a serious leg problem that almost ended his career. These two caught the world's attention. Together they won the race! Hollywood even made a movie about them, called *Champion*, in 1984.

### FACT BOX

Dick Francis was an award-winning jockey. He won 350 races, and rode in eight Grand Nationals. In 1957, he retired and became an award-winning writer. Most of his books are mysteries, set in the world of horse racing. His experience as a jockey gave him great raw material!

*Dick Francis still loves horses. He can often be found around stables, researching or just saying hello.*

# Facts and Figures

By now, you know the sport of steeplechase is full of record-breakers, history-makers, and more than a few risk-takers. Here are some Grand National fascinating facts that have helped make steeplechase the sport it is!

Liam Treadwell was the jockey who rode winner Mon Mome at the John Smith's Grand National on Saturday April 4, 2009. It was Liam's first-ever Grand National! What a way to start!

The more horses racing in the Grand National, the more risk of injury!

The most successful Grand National jockey is George Stevens. In the 1800s, he rode winning horses a record-breaking five times. So far, the fastest time in the Grand National is 8 minutes, 47.8 seconds. That record is held by a horse named Mr. Frisk who ran in 1990. The oldest horse to win the Grand National was named Peter Simple, in 1883. He was 15 years old.

Several horses have won at the young age of 5. These include Alcibiade, Regal, Austerlitz, Empress, and Lutteur III. The number of horses competing in the Grand National has varied over the years. The highest number of racing horses at the Grand National was 66 in 1929. The lowest number is ten, from the Grand National of 1883.

Liam Treadwell celebrates his happiness at winning the 2009 John Smith's Grand National Handicap at Aintree, England.

# Glossary

**bloodlines** The family tree, or "pedigree" of a horse

**euthanized** Killing a hopelessly sick or injured animal

**furlongs** A measurement of 1/8 of a mile, or about 200 meters

**gait** The way a horse or person moves its legs

**hand** Used when measuring a horse, equal to 4 inches (10 cm)

**handicap** A burden placed on a favorite to make the sport more equal

**jockey** A person who rides a horse

**mare** A mature female horse, donkey, or zebra

**martingale** Part of the harness, used to hold down the horse's head

**mentor** A coach, supporter, or teacher who offers advice

**shadow roll** A piece of fabric on a horse's bridle that blocks shadows

**sire** The father of an animal (e.g. horse)

**stallion** A male horse used for breeding

**tack** The name given to the common equipment a horse wears

**withers** The space between a horse's shoulder and neck

# Index

Printed in the U.S.A.—CG